The School of Life:
How to Get Married

First published in 2018 by The School of Life
First published in the USA in 2019
This paperback edition published in 2023
930 High Road, London, N12 9RT

Copyright © The School of Life 2023

Designed and typeset by Marcia Mihotich
Printed and bound in Great Britain by Clays Ltd,
Elcograf S.p.A.

A proportion of this book has appeared online at
www.theschooloflife.com/articles

Every effort has been made to contact the copyright
holders of the material reproduced in this book.
If any have been inadvertently overlooked, the publisher
will be pleased to make restitution at the earliest
opportunity.

The School of Life is a resource for helping us
understand ourselves, for improving our relationships,
our careers and our social lives – as well as for helping
us find calm and get more out of our leisure hours.
We do this through creating films, workshops, books,
apps and gifts.

www.theschooloflife.com

ISBN 978-1-915087-07-2

10 9 8 7 6 5 4 3 2 1

The School of Life:
How to Get Married

The foundations for a lasting relationship

The School of Life

Introduction

1.   Before

2.   The Marriage Service

3.   After

Around the world, different countries have different requirements about what should be said in a legally accepted marriage service. Some countries prescribe a certain set of words, others leave it to the couple but then require a legal procedure in a government office. Do be sure to check the principles at work in your particular jurisdiction.

Introduction

i. The Enduring Point of Marriage

Many of us find it ever harder to know what the point of marriage might be. The drawbacks are evident and well charted. Marriage is a state-sanctioned legal construct, fundamentally linked to matters of property, progeny and pension entitlements – a construct that aims to restrict and control how two people might feel towards one another over fifty or more years. It places a cold, unhelpful, expensive and emotionally alien frame around what will always be a private matter of the heart. We don't need a marriage certificate to show affection and admiration. Indeed, forcing commitment only increases the danger of eventual inauthenticity and dishonesty. If love doesn't work out, being married simply makes it much harder to disentangle two lives and prolongs the agony of a dysfunctional union. Love either works or it doesn't; marriage doesn't help matters one iota either way. It is completely reasonable to suppose that the mature, modern and logical move is to sidestep marriage entirely, along with the obvious nonsense of a wedding.

It would be hopeless to try to defend marriage on the grounds of its convenience. It is clearly cumbersome, expensive, risky and, at junctures, wholly archaic. But that is the point. The whole rationale of marriage is to function as a prison that it is very hard and very embarrassing for two people to get out of.

The essence of marriage is to tie our hands, to frustrate our wills, to put high and costly obstacles in the way of splitting up and sometimes to force two unhappy people to stay in each other's company for longer than either of them would wish. Why do we do this?

Originally, we told ourselves that God wanted us to stay married. But even now, when God looms less large in the argument, we keep making sure that marriage is hard to undo. For one thing, we carefully invite everyone we know to watch us proclaim that we will stick together. We deliberately invite an elderly aunt or uncle whom we don't even like that much to fly around the world to be there. We willingly create a huge layer of embarrassment were we ever to turn round and admit it might have been a mistake. Furthermore, even though we could keep things separate, marriage tends to mean deep economic and legal entanglements. We know it would take a phalanx of accountants and lawyers to prise us apart. It can be done, of course, but it would be ruinous.

It is as if we recognise that there might be some quite good, though strange-sounding, reasons to make it hard to get out of a public life-long commitment to someone else.

Impulse is dangerous

The Marshmallow Test was a celebrated experiment in the history of psychology designed to measure children's ability to delay gratification and track the consequences of being able to think long-term. Some 3-year-olds were offered a marshmallow, but were told they would get two if they held off from eating the first one for five minutes. It turned out a lot of children couldn't make it through this period. The immediate benefit of gobbling the single marshmallow in front of them was stronger than the strategy of waiting for the larger reward. Crucially, it was observed that these children went on to have lives blighted by a lack of impulse control and fared much worse than the children who were best at subordinating immediate fun for long-term benefit.

Relationships are no different. Here too, many things feel urgent. Not eating marshmallows, but escaping, finding freedom, running away, possibly with the new office recruit … Sometimes, we are angry and we want to get out very badly. We are excited by a stranger and want to abandon our present partner at once. And yet, as we look around for the exit, every way seems blocked. It would cost a fortune; it would be embarrassing; it would take an age.

Marriage is a giant inhibitor of impulse set up by our conscience to keep our libidinous, naive, desiring selves in check. What we are essentially buying into by submitting to its dictates is the insight that we are (as individuals) likely to make poor choices under the sway of strong short-term impulses. To marry is to recognise that we require structure to insulate ourselves from our urges. It is to lock ourselves up willingly, because we acknowledge the benefits of the long term, the wisdom of the morning after the storm.

Marriage proceeds without constant reference

to the moods of its protagonists. It isn't about feeling. It is a declaration of intent that is crucially impervious to our day-to-day desires. It is a very unusual marriage in which two people don't spend a notable amount of time fantasising that they weren't in fact married. But the point of marriage is to make these feelings not matter very much. It is an arrangement that protects us from what we desire and yet know (in our more reasonable moments) that we don't truly need or want.

We grow and develop gradually

At their best, relationships involve us in attempts to develop, mature and become 'whole'. We are often drawn to people precisely because they promise to edge us in the right direction.

But the process of our maturation can be agonisingly slow and complicated. We spend long periods (decades, perhaps) blaming the other person for problems that arise from our own weaknesses. We resist attempts at being changed, naively asking to be loved 'for who we are'.

It can take years of supportive interest, many tearful moments of anxiety and much frustration before genuine progress is made. With time, after maybe 120 arguments on a single topic, each party may begin to see it from the other's point of view. Slowly we start to gain insights into our own madness. We find labels for our issues; we give each other maps of our difficult areas; we become a little easier to live with.

Unfortunately, the lessons that are most important for us – the lessons that most contribute to our increasing wisdom and rounded completeness as people – are almost always the most painful to learn. They involve confronting our fears, dismantling our defensive armour, feeling properly guilty about our capacity to hurt another, being genuinely sorry for our faults and learning to put up with someone else's imperfections.

It is too easy to seem kind and normal when we keep starting new relationships. The truth about us, on the basis of which self-improvement can begin, only becomes clear over time. Chances of development can increase hugely when we stay put and don't succumb to the temptation to run away to people who will falsely reassure us that there's nothing too wrong with us.

Investment requires security

Many of the most worthwhile projects require immense sacrifices from both parties, and it's in the nature of such sacrifices that we are most likely to make them for people who are also making them for us.

Marriage is a means by which people can specialise – perhaps in making money or in running a home. This can be hugely constructive. But it carries a risk. Each person (especially if one person stays at home) needs to be assured that they will not later be disadvantaged by their devotion.

Marriage sets up the conditions in which we can

take valuable decisions about what to do with our lives that would be too risky outside of its guarantees.

* * *

Over time, the argument for marriage has shifted. It is no longer about external forces having power over us: churches, the state, the legal idea of legitimacy, the social idea of being respectable ...

What we correctly focus on now is the psychological point of making it hard to throw it all in. It turns out that we benefit greatly (though at a price) from having to stick with certain commitments, because some of our key needs have a long-term structure.

For the last fifty years, the burden of intelligent effort has been on attempting to make separation easier. The challenge now lies in another direction: in trying to remind ourselves why immediate flight doesn't always make sense, in trying to see the point of holding out for the second marshmallow.

Tethering ourselves to our partner, via the public institution of marriage, gives our unavoidable fluctuations of feeling less power to destroy a relationship – one that we know, in calmer moments, is supremely important to us. The point of marriage is to be usefully unpleasant – at least at crucial times. Together we embrace a set of limitations on one kind of freedom – the freedom to run away – so as to protect and strengthen another kind of freedom: a shared ability to mature and create something of lasting value, one whose pains are aligned to our better selves.

ii. The Point of a Wedding Ceremony

The spirit of our times is firmly against ceremony. If we charted a line across the ages, we would see a decline, starting slowly in the mid-18th century and accelerating rapidly through the 20th, away from protocol, etiquette, propriety and all aspects of solemn ritual towards a relaxed, informal spontaneity.

The change is easiest to see in attitudes towards manners and clothing. It was once widely held that people should be seated at dinner parties in order of social rank; it was scandalous to use the wrong cutlery; people would regularly bow to one another; 'sir' and 'madam' were normal words; a waistcoat was an essential part of elegant male attire; women would always wear gloves; children would not speak to adults unless invited to. Now we all wear jeans and say 'hi'.

Very few elaborate ceremonies have survived: marriage is one of them. Here we tend to remain as ritualistic as our ancestors. We put on strange clothes, use antiquated words and spend (perhaps) the price of a small family car on a few hours of rigmarole.

Why do we bother?

The essence of ceremonies is an attempt to mark out an event from the flow of ordinary life. At moments of ritual, we deliberately wear clothes we wouldn't normally be seen in; we carefully speak in ways that are very unlike ordinary conversation; we are directed to do things we'd never otherwise do: pour water over the head of a fully clothed baby, purchase a pair of doves and set them free or eat a seeded rice cake while intoning a poem about the moon's luminosity. The words, clothes and actions are deliberately odd so as to isolate them from ordinary events.

In modern times, there has been an understandable keenness to reduce the oddity of ceremonies. The wish has been to make them more accessible, more normal and less jarring to contemporary sensibilities. There have been attempts to get the participants to speak more colloquially, to wear everyday clothes and to behave as they might in a kitchen. But this is to misunderstand the point of ceremony itself. There are occasions and events that try to mark genuinely radical turning points that sit above everyday life: someone has just arrived on the planet; somebody has just left it; a child is turning into an adult … This is not the everyday. In a marriage ceremony, you are trying on a single day, at a single instant, to commit yourself to another person for the rest of your existence. The event is trying to make an extraordinary leap: to take us out of normal time and put us in touch with something close to eternal. It is trying to defy the ordinary flux of experience, in which circumstances change constantly and passing whims and fancies enjoy complete sway and shepherd us towards a commitment that will last until we are laid out in the grave.

Ceremonies often try to bridge a gap between what might be called the phenomenal and the noumenal. The phenomenal is what we can see, hear and touch: it is the stuff of ordinary experience. The noumenal refers to ideas and events that transcend the day-to-day; we can't easily pin them down at any one moment and yet they are permanently and crucially in the background. For example, traditional ceremonies around naming a baby stress the noumenal: they are saying, in effect, that certain letters appended to a soft young body will always be that person's name. It will still be their name when they are a teenager on a dance floor, a middle-aged executive on the way to a conference and an elderly grandparent drinking chamomile tea on the terrace of a hotel overlooking the sea in eighty-five years' time. The naming ceremony needs to create a setting of unusual dignity and solemnity to capture the surreal aspect of what is at stake.

Around marriage, the stakes are similarly high. There's a phenomenal moment when the wedding is actually conducted: 2.30 p.m., perhaps, on the 8th of April, when it is just starting to rain and the caterers are shifting trays of hors d'oeuvres into the marquee and by chance a plane bound for Bergen is flying overhead. It is a specific moment in time. But there is also a noumenal meaning; this is for the whole of your life. The event is in the eternal present. It stands outside of time; it won't date. You'll be as much married in twenty-six years' time as you are the moment you make your vows. You are doing this forever.

Maison Carrée, Nîmes, France, built c. 2nd century CE

Traditionally, ceremonial places have taken great pains to enforce the notion of a threshold: the point at which one passes from the everyday to the eternal.

For instance, the Roman temple known as the Maison Carrée at Nîmes in the south of France has a grand flight of steps and a row of magisterial columns that cut off the sacred inner space from the busy public realm. One would not have been allowed to enter the temple itself without first washing, putting on a formal cloak and saying a few words to start a process of spiritual purification.

Similarly, in St Paul's Cathedral in London, the high altar, beyond a quietly emphatic braided crimson rope, is both majestic and off limits. Only on the most significant occasions, such as a wedding, might one be invited to step onto the low raised platform below the altar.

In every culture, the marriage ceremony has special details that mark it out from ordinary time. In Poland,

St Paul's Cathedral High Altar, London, UK, built 1675

the couple often hand-deliver invitations to the wedding (rather than sending an email). After the event, they are given ritual presents of bread and salt to symbolise the nourishing and challenging aspects of the institution to which they have committed themselves. At Shinto weddings in Japan, the bride and groom each take three sips from three different cups of sake and then recite lines from a medieval text about their duties to one another. In the Philippines, the couple release a pair of doves at an appointed moment. In South Korea, the bride and groom frequently present each other with a wooden model of a goose. Before a Berber wedding in Morocco, the bride will wash herself in water transported in buckets by the groom's family from a river at least three valleys away.

Marriage rituals may vary a great deal, but the point is always the same: they signal to everyone, especially the participants, that something very significant is unfolding. The point of these ceremonies is ultimately less tied up to specific actions as it is with getting us to appreciate the transcendent oddity of what is happening.

In almost all countries, it is customary to invite lots of people – which will mean, by definition, lots of people one doesn't especially care for or even like. Here too there is a point. To get married is to commit oneself to doing things for other people: one's spouse initially, but also, in time, perhaps children, parents-in-law and so on. Inviting a grumpy uncle one hasn't seen in a mercifully long time symbolises an acceptance of a responsibility to more than just the movements of one's own heart. Through marriage, we are outgrowing our primary and very understandable (and at points important) selfishness.

Weddings are undoubtedly surreal occasions. But rather than scoff at their oddities, we can learn to see and use them in a serious and strategic way: to try to impress upon our naturally intermittent and casual minds the momentous fact that we are seeking to transform our metaphysical status from two separate individuals to a couple whose fates will be intertwined in ever more intimate ways for the rest of our lives.

iii. The Ceremony

In the past, invoking God was the most impressive and powerful way of signalling the importance of anything: a battle, the collection of the harvest, the start of work on a new building.

Weddings were also emphatically religious events. A couple weren't just promising things to one another; they were making a promise in front of a divine being who, on their death, would judge the worth of their efforts. Religions helped us properly recognise the gravity and strangeness of the act of marriage.

Today, we probably don't see marriage in explicitly religious terms, and this presents us with a conundrum. If we are interested in marriage ceremonies, we have little choice but to use a set of rituals drawn from religion – although their original meanings are liable to leave us cold. We may want to capture the noumenal meaning of getting married, but the only people offering us this possibility wrap it up in a lot of deeply implausible theological speculation.

Our conundrum is the result of a historical process that we might call 'bad secularisation'. Traditionally, religions did two distinctive things. On the one hand, they preached ideas about life after death and the creation of the cosmos. On the other hand, they provided potent rituals for marking the great events of our lives. They continually invited us into noumenal time: in baptism, in marriage, at funerals, on certain special holy days. They commissioned art and architecture specifically designed to take us out of the present moment and to give us a perspective on our existence as a whole.

Secularism proceeded by disputing the big theological claims. But at the same time – and without thinking about it very much – secularism also stripped away the psychologically helpful rituals that happened to have become embedded in the faiths. When secularism threw away the bathwater of theology, it threw away the baby of ceremony. It supposed that because religions had been the guardians of ceremony, we couldn't any longer need or legitimately want profound and elevated rituals to help us at the great moments of our lives. But at its heart, ceremony isn't essentially tied to religious faith; noumenal time – in which we see our lives as a whole – doesn't have to rely on convictions about God speaking to Moses on a mountain or the soul surviving the death of the body.

The task of good secularisation is to steal from the ceremonial techniques of religions while disregarding their explicit theological content. Religions have intermittently been the holders of many genuinely helpful, creative, interesting and wise ideas that shouldn't be left only to those who happen to believe in the surrounding theology. The priority is to rescue what is still inspiring and relevant from all that is no longer easy to believe.

In this book, we will describe in detail a wedding ceremony that uses unusual language, special actions and peculiar rituals to place it outside phenomenal time, in order to help us enter the noumenal space of a life-changing event. Crucially, it contains no theology. The ceremony seeks to learn the underlying insight of religion without leaning on its superstitions. We believe that a wedding should use unfamiliar words; it should (ideally) be in a building that speaks of eternity; the celebrant should be a little imposing; we should wear clothes distinct from our normal attire; we should admit our failings and grasp the failings of the other (and yet still both be willing to share a life). We should, in short, be reminded that we are doing something out of the ordinary, which is at once potentially very good for us, for society and for future generations, yet genuinely terrifying and grave as well.

1

Before

We know that weddings need a huge amount of preparation; we're simply selective in our assessment of where our efforts should be directed. We overwhelmingly interpret the task in logistical terms. We worry a lot about the flowers and devote extraordinary attention to the seating plan. Yet, when people look back on a collapsed union and wonder where the mistakes might have arisen, they rarely conclude that the fault lay in an ill-judged floral display or an unsuccessful after-party.

The main preparation we need is not practical, but philosophical. We need to understand ourselves, our partners, the institution of marriage and the nature of love. We need properly to fathom what we are heading into and what the correct mindset for the journey might be.

What follow are some of the thoughts that a couple should, alongside practical concerns, be turning over in their minds in the months before they cross the threshold into marriage.

i. Acknowledgement of One's Fallible Nature

The idea that one is, in many ways, an extremely difficult person to be around – and hence to be married to – may sound improbable and even offensive. Yet fully understanding and readily and graciously admitting to this possibility might be the best way of making sure one is an endurable proposition over the long term. There are few people more deeply insufferable than those who don't, at regular intervals, suspect they might be so.

All of us are hugely tricky propositions. We don't need to know anyone in particular to know this about everyone. In one way or another, we have all been inadequately parented; we have a panoply of unfortunate psychological traits; we are beset by bad habits; we are anxious, jealous, ill-tempered and vain. We will bring an awesome amount of trouble into someone else's life by agreeing to be their spouse.

We tend to be shielded from this unwelcome news prior to marriage through a mixture of sentimentality and neglect. Our parents loved us too much to tell us; our friends don't want to get bogged down in detailed critiques of our personalities; our exes were too keen to escape from us to break down our flaws – they simply said they needed more space, or a long trip to India.

Furthermore, when we're on our own, we don't notice how annoying we might be in the eyes of others. Perhaps we were sulking for the whole of a Sunday, but no one was there to be driven crazy by our self-pity and passive fury. We may have tendencies to use our work as an escape from intimacy, but so long as we are not permanently with someone, we can pass off our eccentric hours without comment. Our peculiar eating habits won't be real until there is another person across the table to register our challenging chewing sounds and shocking ingredient combinations.

Eventually, a partner will call us out on these traits. It feels like a horrible personal attack that a nicer person would not put us through. But it is no such thing. It is an inevitable response to our failings, which anyone would eventually need to bring up.

Our partner is not really doing anything odd; they are merely holding up a mirror. Seen close up, everyone has an appalling amount wrong with their character. It's not us: it's the human condition. The specifics vary, of course; people are nightmarish in different ways. But the basic point is shared. Whatever we think or feel about ourselves, we will be revealed as sorely defective upon close-up, prolonged inspection. Sadly, it's not that our partner is being too critical or unusually demanding. They are the bearer of inevitable news: that we are a nightmare.

This view of human nature can seem shocking, but only because we're unprepared for it, and therefore tend to assume that it must be a prelude to a constantly fractious relationship. It is nothing of the sort. It is the only reliable basis upon which harmony can be established.

Traditionally, the notion of Original Sin was the

starting point for thinking about ourselves as essentially messed up creatures. The idea emerged at the end of the Roman Empire in the West. As the Empire collapsed in anarchic violence, the major thinker of the era, St Augustine, started to look around for an explanation for the miserable condition of society. His key suggestion was that human nature is essentially flawed and misguided. He identified this failing as 'original' – that is, as part of the basic inheritance of being born human.

Although Original Sin was developed in theological terms, its implication is really psychological: as individuals we have to accept from the outset that there will be quite a lot wrong with us. This shouldn't be seen as a shocking, awkward admission, but as a necessary truth that applies to everyone and must be accepted with humility. It shouldn't be odd to admit our substantial imperfections: on the contrary, it should be ridiculous and suspicious to pretend we might not have any.

Augustine's point remains valid, even though we don't now explain it by the story of the original mother of humanity, Eve, eating a forbidden apple in the Garden of Eden. Our failings have natural, and pretty much unavoidable, origins: our wayward impulses, unreasonable stubbornness, tendency to procrastinate; moodiness, rash decisions, flashes of misdirected anger and arrogance; zones of coldness, panicked responses, bad habits, sterile fussiness, greediness and prickly defensiveness (to start the list). We were born vulnerable; we were haphazardly parented; our brains are not well adapted for self-knowledge; our instincts evolved for a life of hunting and gathering rather than for the demands of modernity; and the culture that surrounds us is frequently alarmist, status-driven and very cruel in demanding success yet ensuring that we will almost always feel like failures. So for entirely different reasons we can embrace the same conclusion as St Augustine: no one has any chance of emerging as an adult without a significant share of serious failings.

The point of all this is to drive home the idea that acknowledging one's flaws isn't a request to admit something very strange. What would be strange would be to think that one was without major defects. Of course, we have some delightful qualities as well. But it does mean that we will unavoidably be very hard for another person to live with. Asking someone to marry you can be a rather cruel thing to do to someone you claim to care about.

The point of becoming clear and honest about our failings is to recognise that we will contribute substantially to the difficulties we are bound to encounter in the marriage. It encourages us to resist the otherwise very tempting thesis that we have married an idiot or a brute. It will help us to smile and say sorry when the other person stands in the kitchen shouting at us, as they will, after another display of our foolishness. With a strong sense of our failings in mind, we'll be more aware of the generosity our partner is displaying in their willingness to take us on.

Ahead of the wedding, therefore, we need to ask ourselves, as candidly as possible, what might be specifically crazy, desperate or undeveloped in ourselves.

Maturity involves having a quite detailed answer to the question: How are you difficult to live with? No one should make vows to another person until they have some proper responses to this primordial enquiry. A presumption of one's own innocence is at the heart of self-righteousness and cruelty.

Because our minds may go blank at this point and remember only our tender and beautiful sides, we can lean on a set of prompts and attempt to answer them as candidly as we can.

When I'm annoyed, I have a tendency to ...

It is hard not to lose one's temper – everyone does it sometimes – but the way we do it might be especially tricky. For instance, we might have a tendency to wildly exaggerate in moments of rage – we know we're blustering and don't truly mean what we say (or shout). But we like to make a drama. Or maybe we simmer below the surface and pretend all is well when we desperately want the other to realise (without our having to tell them) that all is very far from fine.

When I feel hurt, I ...

One's bruised self-regard can manifest in what, to one's

partner, are hard-to-read ways. Perhaps one withdraws: it looks like cold indifference, but it's really self-protection. Or one becomes fanatically industrious and demanding or snide or morose or boastful (as a way of trying to counteract a feeling of vulnerability). The other doesn't know the roots of our behaviour: they are just exposed to the outward performance.

When I'm tired, I …

In principle, tiredness is an innocuous problem: nothing is deeply wrong; we just need a good night's sleep. But the way we behave when tired may seem to tell a different story. Maybe we get snappy or weepy or gloomy or a touch manic. Any of these might worry our partner, who won't automatically know we're just exhausted.

My friends could be a problem in so far as …

These are people we've known perhaps since long before we met our partner; they may bring out sides of our character that are not to the fore in our relationship or marriage; they may even not much like our partner. But it's not readily obvious to us that this can be a problem: we like our friends and we like our partner, and, without thinking about it very much, we imagine that we can all get along just fine. Perhaps we can't.

Around money, I can be difficult because …

Money inevitably brings out stranger aspects in us, but they are so familiar to us we might not notice how odd and troubling they could look to someone who shares our economic life. Perhaps we are exceedingly cautious and conservative; a crisis seems always around the corner; we're terrified of even a small extra expenditure. Maybe (for very deep, intimate reasons) we can't bear to pay much attention to our finances; or we're always looking to the next scheme, or we're extremely hopeful about our future earnings (perhaps with little evidence). Such attitudes feel natural to us but won't necessarily make sense to someone else who comes to the issue via their own equally unique and obscure path.

I guess I worry a lot about …

We've lived for so long with our worries that they feel second nature to us. But to our partner they may be very far from being obvious things to get anxious about. Even after quite a long time together, it might seem strange to them that we become so agitated about a mispronounced word or a routine financial check-up. They don't know the underlying worries, and what drives our worries, unless we are clear about them in our own heads and are able to explain them with all the calm eloquence we can muster.

I'm unusually obsessed by …

Our own obsessions strike us as hugely reasonable and proper. For instance, we might take the view that it matters immensely that the chairs are arranged symmetrically in a room; it's obvious that all the kitchen utensils have to match; clearly, we feel, no intelligent person could think you need to use a chopping board just to cut a loaf of bread; we think it's natural to visit eight art galleries on holiday. We're typically blind to our own obsessions, because they don't feel obsessive. They have profound origins in our past and our character, but they aren't obvious to our partner, who has lived an entirely different life from us up to now. It's hard but crucial to try to get some perspective on the ways in which we might be bringing a very personal and (to be frank) rather odd set of expectations into our shared life.

I've got some routines that I guess can be difficult …

Maybe I have to file my toenails, do several stretching exercises, floss my teeth for three minutes and apply anti-wrinkle cream to my forehead before I can think of getting into bed – though my partner may interpret this as reluctance to join them. Maybe I find it necessary to wash up as much as I can before having dinner, though my partner is eager to eat as soon as the meal is ready. Perhaps over the years I've honed a travel routine – least possible baggage, packed while the taxi is waiting, arriving just before check-in closes. We don't intuitively grasp how off-putting or maddening our own routines might be for a partner; they hardly even strike us as routines, as they just seem natural and right. And that, of course, is where the problem lies: with insufficient attention to our basic strangeness.

* * * *

The point of prompting greater awareness of our own questionable patterns of behaviour isn't to feel guilty or ashamed about them, but to see how easily they could be confusing, disturbing and annoying to another person. Before we commit ourselves to marriage, we need to become fully acquainted with all the ways in which we might be a serious challenge to be around.

ii. The Imperfection of the Other

It sounds deeply unromantic – especially in the lead-up to a wedding – to devote sustained attention to the flaws of one's partner. At this stage we're supposed to be entranced by all that is admirable about a future spouse. Yet getting a clear-eyed and penetrating view of the failings of the person one shares one's life with is perhaps the kindest and most love-sustaining thing we can do. This is because the success or failure of a relationship doesn't hinge on whether another person is flawed: they definitely are. What matters is how we interpret their failings; how we understand the reasons why they have in the past been and will in the future be very difficult to be with. The crux is whether we can move from interpreting their annoying sides as signs that they are mean or mad to viewing them as symptoms of pain and anxiety. We will have learnt to love when our default response to unfortunate behaviour is not to feel aggrieved that our right to happiness is under threat but to wonder what aspects of a partner's damaged past have been engaged.

At our more fragile moments, it is clear where our partner's failings come from: wilful awfulness. They are the expression of an almost devilish desire to humiliate and distress us. If they're less sexually intense than we'd like them to be, or too pushy around sex, or too messy, fussy, argumentative or lacking in interesting opinions, we interpret this as something they could easily change if they wanted to. It is just that they can't be bothered;

they're being selfish and wilfully wrecking our chances of happiness.

But the truth is almost invariably very different. Our partner's annoying characteristics have their roots in childhood, long before they met us. They emerged as strategies for coping with the stresses of their early years. Perhaps an over-critical, demanding mother made them feel as if being a bit disorganised and untidy was a necessary rebellion: a crucial assertion of independence that left them with an enduring sense that hanging up their clothes neatly or keeping the kitchen surfaces pristine could be of interest only to a tyrant. Their behaviour today may be exasperating, but they're not evil: they're just playing out the legacy of a difficult aspect of their lives when they were little.

Maybe they grew up in a family that didn't feel socially secure: now they are keen to spend as much money as possible; they have a tendency to show off; they're overly impressed by people you don't much admire; they want to go to parties all the time and make a fuss if they don't think you look smart enough. The surface behaviour gets to you, but this flaw can be more charitably seen as an attempt to compensate for what they experienced as the humiliations of their upbringing. They may never properly admit this to you, but instead of merely hating this side of their character, you can understand it and partly forgive it in the light of its origins. They are not simply a bit snobbish; they are attempting (as best they can) to escape certain past miseries.

A partner's less appealing sides can almost always be understood as responses to background fears and worries. If they seem lazy, it could be because their deep love of perfection leaves them terrified of making a mistake. If they are sulky, it may be because they fear they cannot make themselves properly understood. If they are short-tempered, this could be due to worries about failure at work, driven on by the ghostly presence of a disapproving father.

Any unpleasing action can be given a more or less charitable interpretation. And odd though it sounds at first, the charitable interpretation is usually right. We instantly recognise this when it comes to ourselves. We know how our own less endearing qualities deserve to be seen not as an expression of our deep nastiness but as responses to fear and anxiety. We know ourselves to be more deserving of pity than condemnation. And since this is true of us, it is very likely to be true of our partner too.

As we embark on marriage, we should accept that we're not going to start liking our partner's worse aspects – and nor should we expect to. We should acknowledge that they almost certainly won't change much. Neither of these points should be decisive. We are ideally ready for marriage not when we have encountered perfection or achieved a sage-like calm, just when we're willing – in our less pressured moments – to give a charitable interpretation to our partner's many failings.

It's helpful, though strange, to become more explicit. We could usefully draw up in our minds a list of the seven most annoying things about our partners. Some might seem embarrassingly trivial, some very substantial. The task is not mean or inappropriate. We're not trying to condemn our partners per se but rather to lay the groundwork for love.

We then need to try to imagine the kindest, most charitable explanation for these annoying characteristics. What things in their past might explain this very tricky habit or obsession or disproportionate, exaggerated worry of theirs? How could a lovely person, under dynamics they didn't ask for, end up being like that? We're imaginatively rehearsing the crucial move from an irate interpretation – which sees a defect as a sign that a person is stupid, mean, heartless or cruel – to a benign, kindly, loving one that sees them as suffering from a past misfortune. Their annoying conduct or mentality doesn't show that they are evil (as we will always think at our most frayed moments), but simply that they are labouring with a difficulty that might deserve compassion.

A charitable interpretation of defects in one's partner doesn't make it lovely to be confronted with their troubles. We are still with someone who thwarts us, is over-critical, clingy or cold, or has a touch of the snob about them. But we're set to be less disgusted and less panicked in the face of these ills. We're strengthening our capacity to stick with them, because we see that their failings don't make them unworthy of love; indeed, they render them all the more urgently in need of it.

Part of this involves overcoming the haunting

feeling that we'd be better off with someone else. After we have been together with someone for a while, a lot of new people will appear to be exciting and kind. We may occasionally meet an example who seems distinctly nicer: they are warmer or funnier or better-looking, a better listener or more interested in the things that fascinate us. The comparison at once casts our partner in a distinctly unflattering light. Why on earth are we contemplating a lifetime with someone so flawed?

Our partners aren't uniquely damaged. We just know them much better than the exciting stranger. Our partner suffers from the disadvantages of incumbency, of having been in our lives for so long that we have seen the full range of their inadequacies. Our certainty that we might be happier with another person is founded on ignorance. It is the result of having been shielded from the worst and more crazy dimensions of a new character's personality, which we must accept will be there – not because we know them in any detail, but because we know the human race, of which (despite their exceptionally pleasing looks and manner) they remain a part.

iii. Why Am I with This Person?

Typically, when asked why we are marrying someone, we feel pressured to respond by listing the ways they are lovely to be with. But a bigger, fairer explanation of why we're with them, and why they might be a good spouse for us, involves exploring three questions: What might I learn from them? In what ways has my past constrained my choice of partner? And what pragmatic or 'low' reasons might I have for getting together with them?

We will look at each in turn.

What we need to learn from our partners

A lot of what drives our search for love is a desire for strengths in a partner – more particularly, strengths that we don't possess ourselves. We picked them because they know how to do and be certain things that elude us.

Our 'weaknesses' – our deficiencies, frailties and imperfections – are crucial components in our excitement around our lover. We love because we are incomplete and unbalanced. We might be over-intellectual and therefore find them delightfully down-to-earth. We may be a bit flighty and chaotic and so think them wonderfully ordered and precise.

My weaknesses	The strengths that attract me
Easily rattled	Calmness, steadfastness
Conformist, rule-bound	Creativity, authenticity
Emotional reserve, inhibition	Warmth, exuberance
Shyness	Confidence
Chaotic	Ordered

Ideally, we want to learn from a lover and become a little more like them. Helped by their central place in our lives, we will become calmer or more confident or more adventurous or better at organising ourselves. The dream is that they will teach us by example and encouragement and that, under the protection of their love, we will grow to our full potential.

This means that the success of the marriage will depend on two things: our willingness to truly learn the lessons on offer, and our partner's readiness to be a good teacher. The trouble is, most of us are not especially good at either side of the equation.

In reality, we often fail to learn from our partner's strengths. It feels humiliating to own up to the many ways in which we're far from perfect. It's annoying to have to make the real changes in our thinking and behaviour that are required. Although theoretically we want to evolve, under pressure, we too often end up feeling our partner should do that infinitely comforting thing: just love us as we are. Because their strengths carry with them a need for evolution, we can start to see them as punishing and nasty. At first we liked their down-to-earth quality, but in time we may denigrate it as naive and simplistic. We may originally have admired their neat and orderly ways, but, when we're struggling, we're inclined to blame them for being rigid, anal and uncreative. When it's painful for us to improve ourselves, we turn on the 'teacher' and accuse them of preventing us from remaining the person we know deep down we shouldn't be any longer.

We're not very good students – and our partner might not be a very adept teacher either. They know plenty of things we could usefully absorb, but they may grow impatient and stern in the way they convey these. They get annoyed by our failings and feel (and might sometimes say) that we are hopeless. When confronted by our hesitancy and inhibitions, they don't become brilliant coaches who carefully lead us by small, manageable steps; they become frustrated and let us know that we're dreary, conformist bores. Around our difficulties with practical matters, they may not sympathetically reduce our anxiety and heap encouraging praise on our tentative efforts. They merely sigh impatiently and tell us to get out of the way because they're obviously going to have to take care of everything themselves.

As a result, we become further entrenched in our pre-existing pattern of strengths and weaknesses. The one who is more financially minded ends up doing everything around money, and the other gets more and more passive around it. The more domestic one ends up doing practically everything around the house; the more creative one comes to feel they have less and less in common with their staid companion.

But we're not condemned to follow this unfortunate path if we have it clear in our heads that a reason for getting married is to learn and to teach. A pedagogical explanation of why we are with someone shows us that we'll have to be gracious enough to admit our failings and adopt the role of a genuine student. At other points, in our role as a teacher, we'll need to avoid getting impatient and self-righteous with our inevitably slow and faltering student. To be married with a degree of success, we will have to accept the nobility and necessity of teaching and learning.

We can't love just anyone

Theoretically, we are free to select the kind of person we marry. We might have chosen someone else. We're not being forced into this by social convention, matchmaking aunts or dynastic imperatives. But in reality our choice is probably much less free than we imagine. Some very real constraints around whom we can love and feel properly attracted to come from a place we might not think to look: our childhoods. Our psychological history strongly predisposes us to fall only for certain types of people.

We love along grooves formed in childhood. We look for people who in many ways recreate the feelings of love we knew when we were small. The problem is that the love we imbibed in childhood was unlikely ever to have been made up simply of generosity, tenderness and kindness. Given the way the world is, love was liable to have come entwined with certain very painful aspects: a feeling of not being good enough; a love for a parent who was fragile or depressed; a sense that one could never be fully vulnerable around a caregiver.

This predisposes us to look in adulthood for partners who won't necessarily simply be kind to us, but who will most importantly feel familiar – a subtly but importantly different thing. We may be constrained to look away from prospective candidates because they don't satisfy a yearning for the complexities we associate with love. We may describe someone as 'not sexy' or 'boring' when in truth we mean 'unlikely to make me suffer in the way I need to suffer in order to feel that love is real'.

It is common to advise people who are drawn to tricky candidates simply to leave them and find someone more wholesome. This is as theoretically appealing as it is practically impossible. We cannot magically redirect the wellsprings of our attraction. Rather than aim for a transformation in the types of people we are attracted to, it may be wiser simply to adjust the way we respond and behave around the occasionally difficult characters whom our past mandates we will find compelling.

Our problems are often generated because we continue to respond to compelling people in the way we learned to behave as children around their templates. For instance, maybe we had an irate parent who often raised their voice. We loved them, and reacted by feeling that when they were angry we must be guilty. We became timid and humble. Now if a partner (to whom we are magnetically drawn) gets cross, we respond as squashed, brow-beaten children: we sulk; we feel it's our fault; we feel got at and yet deserving of criticism; we build up a lot of resentment. Or if we had a fragile, vulnerable parent who was easily hurt, we readily end up with a partner who is also a bit weak and demands that we care for them, but then we get frustrated by their weakness – we tiptoe around them, we try to encourage and reassure (as we did when we were little), but we also condemn this person for being undeserving.

We probably can't change our templates of attraction. But rather than seek to radically re-engineer our instincts, we can try to learn to react to them not as we did as children but in the more mature and constructive manner of a rational adult. There is an enormous opportunity to move ourselves from a childlike to a more adult pattern of response in relation to the difficulties to which we are attracted. (*See table on page 55.*)

We are almost certainly with somebody who has a particularly knotty set of issues that trigger both our desires and our childlike defensive moves. The answer isn't to end the relationship, but rather to strive to deal with the challenges of our partner with wisdom of which we weren't capable when we first encountered these in a parent or caregiver. It probably isn't in our remit to locate a wholly grown-up person, but it is always in our power to strive to behave in more grown-up ways around our partner's less mature sides.

A: Partner's tricky behaviour	B: Childlike response on our part	C: More adult response we should aim for
Raising voice	*'It's all my fault...'*	*'This is their issue: I don't have to feel bad.'*
Patronising	*'I'm stupid.'*	*'There are lots of kinds of intelligence. Mine is fine.'*
Morose	*'I have to fix you.'*	*'I'll do my best, but I'm not responsible for your mindset, and this doesn't have to impact on my self-esteem ...'*
Overbearing	*'I deserve this.'*	*'I'm not intimidated by you.'*
Distracted, preoccupied	*'Notice me.'*	*'You're busy, I'm busy, that's OK ...'*

Romantic vs. pragmatic motives

There are many reasons why we might be planning to build a life with someone. But within our culture, not all reasons are deemed equal. We could divide our motives into the categories of the Romantic and the pragmatic. (*See table on page 58.*)

At present, our culture hugely favours the Romantic reasons, and leaves us to feel guilty and soiled around the pragmatic ones. It can be shameful to think that a major motive for marrying someone is that we find them extremely attractive. Or to recognise that if they didn't have their present income, the pull would be far less intense. We would be unlikely to admit to a friend that we were thrilled to be joining our lives with someone who had admirably compatible views on how to keep a kitchen.

But that is only because we are in denial about who we really are. We are creatures who delight in the union of two hearts, who long to find our feelings of melancholy and purpose reflected in the eyes of another and who have tender and vast thoughts under star-filled skies late on Saturday nights. However, we also have our nine-on-Monday-morning identities, when we are practical, resolute, uninclined to pathos and flights of fancy and highly appreciative of punctuality and good order.

A sound marriage requires an adroit blend of romantic and practical sympathies. Much of what we are attempting to do will rely on logistical talents that support rather than undermine our romantic concerns. The point of having a bit of money is to enable us to stop thinking about it all the time. The point of an ordered house is to prevent us having to spend too many hours rooting around at the backs of cupboards. Our lives become a lot more boring when we stubbornly refuse to pay any attention to 'boring things'.

Furthermore, agreement on pragmatic issues can sustain us when agreement on romantic ones proves elusive. It is easy to lose patience with someone's soul, but perhaps harder to lose sight of the importance of clean linen or a reassuringly administered bank account. Prosaic, materialistic thoughts are there to help us stay together while we learn to cope more maturely with the emotional conflicts that accompany us through our lives.

A marriage is a deeply practical project. It is akin to an attempt to run a small business together, one that involves property law, catering, holiday tours, entertainment, kindergarten management and home decoration. If we insist on seeing our partner's organisational skills, financial acumen or prowess as a host as simply 'low', we won't recognise the very genuine contributions these assets might make to our existence.

It is strategically useful to get more explicit about identifying the most pragmatic reasons why we have picked our partner, and perhaps to sum these up in a (secret) list we keep in a bedside drawer. Ideally we'd return to the list at points of crisis in order to remind ourselves of just why we ended up choosing as we did, until such time as we succeed in recovering admiration for, and connection to, our partner's soul.

Romantic reasons for marriage	Pragmatic reasons for marriage
Mutual sympathy and tenderness	We like the same kind of furniture/house design
Soulmates: they understand the poetry of our hearts	We have similar attitudes to child raising
They understand our sadness	We will have financial security
They finish our sentences	We will have status among our social group
The same music touches us both	We like each other's views on films

iv. Dark Premeditations

It is customary to be upbeat when a marriage is announced. Society wants to stress how happy the couple will be; it tries to raise their spirits and build up their hopes. This feels like a kind and generous thing to do, but in reality, optimism has some hugely unfortunate consequences. It means that central aspects of the reality of a shared life will come as a brutal disappointment, for which a couple will be unprepared and to which they are liable to react with bitterness and fury. Carefully wielded pessimism turns out to be one of the greatest gifts of contented couples.

In a wiser culture, people entering marriage would be strongly encouraged to contemplate the sorrows likely to come their way. This wouldn't stop them getting together; it would correctly ready them for what they were trying to do. If two people were going to start on an expedition up an extremely high mountain, it would be neither kind nor useful for a guide to suggest the climb would be undemanding when, in reality, they were going to be facing ice walls, over-hangs, exhaustion, minus-forty-degree nights and cataclysmic storms sweeping in without warning from innocent blue skies.

When things get tough in a marriage, the greatest temptation is to feel that the difficulties stem from having chosen the wrong partner. If we are guided by an underlying optimism around what marriage is supposed to be like, we will stay loyal to our naive ideas of love while growing highly disloyal to the particular lover with whom we have attempted to enact them.

To inoculate ourselves against curdled sentimentality, we need to perform a series of exercises, termed 'pre-meditations', which systematically investigate the darker scenarios we may have to face. These are not to be confused with predictions: considering them doesn't make them happen, it simply renders us grateful if we skirt them. A good marriage isn't one free of difficulties; it is one in which the difficulties have been factored in, have been understood to stem from the inherent complexities of what is being attempted and are not interpreted by either party as a violation of a beatific original contract.

Money

Money will always be trouble. It is impossible that it won't be, because money is never just about money: it is an ultimate symbol of affection. Even if there is technically money in a joint account, there can still be an intense feeling of having been robbed when a relationship is under stress. Any feeling of being emotionally neglected can become identified with financial ebbs and flows. It is almost impossible to be in a committed relationship and not, at some level, be facing periods of anxiety or quiet rage around cash.

The standard advice tends to be procedural and sunny: we are told to be transparent, to keep receipts and to open a shared accounts book in which we both jot down expenses. It won't work – not because we are with the wrong person, but because money is fiendishly linked to the broader spectrum of our psychology. Thanks to our background and past experience, we might see money as the key mark of dignity, or as utterly unrelated to what is truly important in life. We may carry the burdens of parents who were overly impressed by wealth or of a family that felt economically humiliated. It is exceptionally unlikely that two people will ever have the same deep and detailed attitudes to money. Therefore, money will very likely become a major point of contention – not because we are with the wrong person but because we are with another person.

The right attitude is to understand that money can't help but be a difficult theme, and not to become too alarmed when conflicts emerge. Crucially, we should not concentrate on the money issues themselves, but seek to grasp why they are so powerful on both sides. We need to see, compassionately and accurately, what their emotional resonance is. We need to investigate our own less than fully conscious psychological legacy. That won't make a shortage of money go away or remove a structural imbalance in resources between two people. But it provides an avenue of understanding. Instead of merely getting angry, we can grasp the conflict as an essential part of what marriage involves. A decent marriage isn't one that has no money angst but one in which two people genuinely try to make sense of the psychological sources of their inevitable financial quirks.

Sex

If extraordinary sex is a priority, we should never get married. The largest generalisation we can make of marriage is that sex will decline within it. This isn't a sign that we have made a mistake, but that we are succeeding at long-term commitment.

Sex rewards adventure, risk, naughtiness, a lack of barriers and novelty. But a good marriage is based around stability, continuity, a degree of guardedness and carefully monitored boundaries.

That is why, over a marriage, we are bound to experience a range of frustrations and let-downs. We and our partner will both be sexually curious about other people, but both be appalled by the possibility of the other's vagabond attention. We will have to keep most of what we imagine and long for secret. We will either feel rejected by their lack of interest or humiliated by the intensity of their demands. Far from being the ideal expression of mutual love, sex will become a battlefield of grievances, reproaches and bitterness. It will, most evenings, feel much easier just to read a book.

What makes sexual conflict far harder to deal with than it should be is the natural but unfair idea that the pain might be someone's fault – perhaps one's own but far more likely one's partner's. In truth, it is not the result of anyone being pointedly awful. The horror arises because of the manifold complications of human sexuality, for which neither party is ever overly responsible.

Childcare

Having children promises us some of the greatest joys of marriage, but also offers us the most reliable route to wrecking a relationship. It vastly expands the range of topics over which two people can argue and feel resentful. It is highly unlikely that one will be able to bring up children one adores without in some way reducing the love one ends up feeling for one's fellow parent.

The reasons are endless. For years (it could be only seven, but it will feel like eternity), it will be almost impossible to sleep or even to think properly. There will be yogurt on the back of the kitchen chairs. There will be anguished moments when a small baby is ill, urgently in need of something, screaming, brightly but oddly coloured – and unable to let on as to what should be done. The intensity of our love for our child will increase the stakes in every disagreement with our spouse: we will find we are at odds over sleeping habits, the role of in-laws, how tolerant or demanding to be, how much ice cream it's acceptable to eat, and how a child should behave in a restaurant. A lot will go wrong with our child and we'll know whom to blame: our partner, who will have been too protective or too careless, too indulgent or too strict, too much in thrall to experts or too rejecting of expert opinion. Instead of our shared love for our child being something that draws us ever more deeply together, it will prove a tortured zone of contention. We'll feel certain that we'd split up if it wasn't for the children – although it's primarily the presence of children that will render the idea of divorce so attractive.

A better and wiser attitude to childcare starts from the idea that we are not attempting to create a perfect human being. We will be far from flawless parents, and this matters not a jot. The mid-20th-century English psychoanalyst Donald Winnicott, who specialised in working with parents and children, was disturbed by how often he encountered in his consulting rooms parents who were deeply disappointed with themselves. They felt they were failing as parents and hated themselves as a result. They were ashamed of their occasional rows, their bursts of short temper, their times of boredom around their own child, their many mistakes. They were haunted by a range of anxious questions: Are we too strict, too lenient, too protective, not protective enough? What struck Winnicott, however, was that these people were almost always not at all bad parents. They were not, by some fantasy ideal, perfect, but they were – as he came to put it, rather wonderfully – 'good enough'.

And 'good enough', strangely, is even better than 'perfect', because a child will need to live the rest of their lives in a very imperfect world. It is good for them to get used to the idea of error early on. The good-enough parent is at times irate, stupid, a bit unfair, rather tired and a touch depressed. And in so being, they are doing something truly valuable for the child: preparing them for reality.

Being entirely honest

For years, you felt burdened with thoughts, feelings and opinions that didn't seem to make much sense to anyone else. There were people you didn't like, but everyone else seemed to think they were terrific, so you held your tongue. There were things you would have liked to try in bed, but they felt shameful and you kept quiet about them. You learnt to have secrets in order to be liked. Then, finally, you met a very special person. What made them so special was that you no longer had to dissemble around them. You could admit to important truths. You could confess, and be rewarded for sharing, your deepest self. It was a favourite game in the early months. You pushed yourself to go as far as you could. The deeper the secret, the better. No area of the self seemed beyond investigation, no secret too shocking or explicit. You could explain that you found a mutual acquaintance arrogant, narcissistic and mean. Or that you thought some supposed 'masterpiece' of a book very boring. You could explain that you liked pulling hair during sex or had always been excited by ropes. Love seemed to be born out of a possibility for new honesty. What had previously been taboo gave way to exhilarating intimacy.

The relief of honesty is at the heart of the feeling of being in love. A sense of mutual conspiracy underlies the touch of pity that every new couple feels for the rest of humanity. But this sharing of secrets sets up in our minds – and in our collective culture – a powerful and potentially problematic ideal: that if two people love one another, they must always tell each other the truth about everything.

The idea of honesty is sublime. It presents a deeply moving vision of how two people can be together, and it is a constant presence in the early months. But there is a problem: we keep wanting to make this same demand as the relationship goes on. And yet in order to be kind, and in order to sustain the relationship over decades, it ultimately becomes necessary to keep a great many thoughts out of sight. We are perhaps too conscious of the bad reasons for hiding something; we haven't paid enough attention to the noble reasons why, from time to time, true loyalty may lead one to say very much less than the whole truth.

We are so impressed by honesty that we have forgotten the virtues of politeness – this word defined not as a cynical withholding of important information for the sake of harm, but as a dedication to not rubbing someone up against the true, hurtful aspects of one's nature. It is ultimately no great sign of kindness to insist on showing someone one's entire self at all times. Repression, a certain degree of restraint and a dedication to editing one's pronouncements belongs to love as much as a capacity for explicit confession. The person who cannot tolerate secrets, who in the name of 'being honest' shares information so wounding it cannot be forgotten, is no friend of love. Just as no parent tells a child the whole truth, so we should accept the ongoing need to edit our full reality. And if one suspects (and one should, rather regularly, if the relationship is a good one) that one's partner might be lying too (about what they are thinking about, about how they judge one's work, about where they were last night), it is perhaps best not to take up arms and lay into them like a relentless inquisitor, however intensely one yearns to do that. It may be kinder, wiser and perhaps more in the true spirit of love to pretend that one simply didn't notice.

v. Loving and Being Loved

We learn about love, initially, by being loved. If things went moderately well in childhood, we have powerful memories of being (at least from time to time) on the receiving end of immense understanding and kindness. And very little was expected in return. Our caregivers didn't assume that – aged 3 or 6 – we could solve their problems; they didn't expect us to listen carefully to their heartaches or shoulder a range of domestic responsibilities; they didn't berate us for not making enough money or for being too materialistic. Often enough, in their eyes we were deeply lovely and they readily embraced the tasks of nurturing our strengths and consoling our woes; in return they only hoped for the occasional hug and sweet smile. We learned a huge amount about what it feels like to be loved.

This childhood experience feels to us like the normal template of a loving relationship. In our eyes, the parent's love was natural and instinctive: of course they were there to pat our head, enquire tenderly and patiently about the little incidents of our day, to cheer us on, to share our troubles and to look after us without asking for us to do the equivalent for them. Largely, the parents carefully shielded us from insight into what their devotion to us cost them. They didn't say that they were on the point of losing their temper with us five times but managed to hold back; they didn't explain that they dropped into bed utterly worn out and depleted; they didn't usually let us see the degree of inner conflict they felt; however much they loved us, they feared they were trading portions of their lives making us sandwiches and calming us down when they should have been building their careers. We didn't know what it was really like for them – and, in a sense, we didn't really care.

In adulthood, we encounter love in the guise of feeling loved. But for a relationship to survive, we need to do something very tricky: we need to become like the parent whose efforts we never understood. We want to be loved, but we have to be loving in return. The pure demand to be loved is disastrous, because no one except a parent can settle for such a degree of inequality. We have to become, at least sometimes, the one who subordinates their desires to the comfort and security of the other; we need to listen, without particularly being listened to; we need to sympathise even though, at the moment, it's all one way; we need to appear charmed even if inside we're a touch bored; we need – perhaps for the first time – to do what a parent did for us and put the interests of another, briefly but truly, ahead of our own. Marriage may be summarised as the project of doing an utterly remarkable thing: surrendering at points our hungry claims to being loved in order to take on the new and unfamiliar burdens of actually loving.

vi. An Emotional Prenuptial Contract

At present, a prenuptial contract typically addresses the division of money and property should a marriage break down. Drawing one up can look rather cynical, but it is a hugely wise move. A prenuptial contract takes seriously the idea that a marriage (however well intentioned at its start) might turn out badly. So it seeks to clarify certain issues in advance, when people are calm and well-disposed – understanding that it will be much harder to resolve contentious matters in the heat of psychological conflict.

But the problem with existing prenuptial contracts isn't that they are cold, heartless documents; it's that they are too narrow in the issues they address. Ideally, there would be six emotional prenuptial clauses that any couple would sign up to before getting married. These wouldn't be focused on the final, extreme problem of how to separate; instead, they would define how each person should ideally see the marriage – and they would aim to increase the chances of a successful long-term relationship through doses of bracing and hard-won realism.

Clause 1: I will give up on perfection

A key indicator that you are ready for marriage is when you properly accept that your partner is deeply and substantially flawed. They are lovely in some ways but also (you clearly see) the carrier of many annoying and unfortunate characteristics; these might shift over time, but they won't all go away, and new zones of troubling oddity will emerge. In multiple ways, they will be difficult to live with. But this insight is balanced by an equally direct recognition that this is completely standard. Seen from close up, everyone is slightly nightmarish in certain aspects. Therefore, one is not miserably accepting an unusually awful partner; one is openly admitting that to be married at all means tying oneself to a problematic fellow human being. A crucial consequence is that one will surrender any lingering illusion that there must be someone better out there. We'll be ready for marriage when we take it for granted that there is no 'right' person for us and won't be tempted to leap to the conclusion that we have married the 'wrong' person.

Clause 2: I do not expect to be fully understood

We have inherited from Romanticism the over-optimistic notion that, in a loving relationship, all the most vulnerable, secret and intricate parts of ourselves can finally be understood and accepted. The other (we like to imagine) gazes into the depths of our souls with a magnificent combination of insight and acceptance. But, however much the other seems to understand us, there will always remain major portions of our inner life that elude and confuse them. Eventually, we're all revealed as a mystery – in some central areas – to everyone else. Our spouse will unavoidably be unable to grasp certain important things about us. They will lack the ideal sympathy we long for – not because they are stupid or cruel, but because they are another, separate individual. We're ready for marriage when we finally give up on the hope, described as Romantic but in reality merely reckless, of being justly and fully comprehended by another human.

Clause 3: I recognise that I'm crazy

In many situations at work or with friends, it may be easy to pass as fair-minded, reasonable, pleasant and easy-going: as a rather sane person. But this can never be the whole truth. In private, you are, evidently, somewhat crazed. You are liable to get out of control, to bear intense grudges, to fixate on things that will strike others as deeply improbable, to succumb to bouts of anxiety that seem to defy common sense. Maturity doesn't mean eliminating all these quirks and troubling tendencies; it means admitting them graciously, regretting them deeply and humbly perceiving how they will be immensely complicated for another person to cope with. Being ready to settle down involves a degree of acute, helpfully deployed embarrassment around who one is.

Clause 4: I am ready to stop wanting to be loved and ready to start loving

Naturally, we want to be loved – and in their fashion our partner does love us. But the test of readiness for marriage isn't how much we long to be on the receiving end of another person's selfless kindness. It means adopting towards our partner something like a parent's attitude to their child. The parent wants to assist, even though they won't get much thanks. They want to comfort, even though they know they won't be comforted in return. They will forgive, despite the fact that their sympathy won't be duly acknowledged. They will be ready to listen more than they are listened to, and won't store this up in a reservoir of resentment. They will actively seek out the charming and endearing sides of their child – especially when they are not obvious. With another adult, we are not easily inclined to do such things. But we're well set for marriage when we're readier to give than to demand love.

Clause 5: I am ready for administration

Our generally Romantic culture foregrounds the role of emotions in relationships. But day to day, over a long period of time together, much of what a couple will have to do together is practical in character. They will be cooking, cleaning, budgeting, occasionally hiring an electrician; they will be making purchasing decisions and deciding what to throw away. If there are children, they will be spending significant portions of their lives ferrying them across the land. These are not in any way Romantic undertakings; there's no glamour attached to them; love songs don't relish the times when we'll finally be paying insurance bills together or drawing up a roster of whose turn it is to empty the pedal bin in the bathroom. Many couples have found themselves deeply disappointed that shared life is governed by chores and administration: that more time is spent on finances and tidying up than is passed in discussion of psychological or metaphysical issues.

We're ready for marriage when we accept the dignity of the ironing board or of the trip to the supermarket: when we have in our sights a realistic idea of how central administration and domestic management are actually going to be – and when we see that this isn't a failure of love, just the natural consequence of the success of love.

Clause 6: I am ready to learn and to teach

We too easily think that love means being accepted as we are and that any attempt to change us must signal malevolence. But it is inevitable that any partner who truly cares for us will want us to be a little different from the way we are. We should good-naturedly accept the role of learning – and teaching.

A couple who freely and frankly agree on these six points can be declared ready for marriage and embark on their new relationship with realistic confidence.

An emotional prenuptial contract

Ideally, the witness should be the marriage director – the person who will conduct the wedding ceremony. A copy of this document should be kept by the couple and exhibited in a place where they can both see it every day at home. It might ideally be framed.

An emotional prenuptial contract between

....

and ....

Dated ....

I freely and openly declare:

Clause 1: I have given up on perfection

Clause 2: I do not expect to be fully understood

Clause 3: I recognise that I'm crazy

Clause 4: I am ready to stop wanting to be loved
and ready to start loving

Clause 5: I am ready for domestic administration

Clause 6: I am ready to learn and to teach patiently

Signed ....

Signed ....

Witness ....

vii. Premarriage Guidance

Ideally, the dark premeditations, the exercises associated with them and the clauses of the prenuptial contract will be explored in a sequence of structured discussions with a marriage director who will eventually lead the ceremony. In a number of sessions, it will be possible to cover the ground under discussion. There is a specific advantage of doing so in the company of someone who can probe our responses and push us, gently but usefully, to greater candour. On our own, we have (whatever our intentions) a devilish capacity for sidestepping the trickier facts about ourselves – which are also the ones it is most helpful to be aware of.

viii. Planning the Ceremony

The desire to have a different sort of marriage (more realistic, honest, resilient and mature) logically inspires a desire for a different sort of wedding ceremony. A full set of instructions follows.

Ahead of the ceremony itself, aside from the obvious practicalities (rings, invitations, after-party), the couple should make two specific preparations:

The Book of Imperfections

The partners should each buy a handsome, solid, empty book and head it 'The Book of Imperfections'. Ensuring that the books are attractive and long-lasting signals their significance for the couple.

Filling in each book will be a matter of many hours. In it, partners should record the severe and deep failings of their characters – as well as they can understand them at the moment – but knowing there are sure to be others, which may possibly be even worse. As a proof of love and trust, they should candidly admit to all that they know is bad about them. Outlined in the book are the broken parts of them, for which they need forgiveness. The idea is to be frightened of – and humbled by – the power this gives the other person.

Typical entries will detail failures of patience, of humour, of insight and of loyalty. The book should contain an honest audit of the darkest sides of the self.

Photographs of the two partners as children

Partners should – in addition – find a representative picture of themselves as children (before adolescence). The picture should in some way endear the viewer, though not in any overtly sentimental or naive way. The point is to be reminded that this big and often rather hard-to-like adult was also once a child.

The presence of this picture should draw the couple – at testing moments – to the memory of their more hopeful and dignified sides.

2
The Marriage Service

i. The Setting

Location

Ideally, the marriage ceremony should take place in a location radically distinct from everyday life, to emphasise its uniqueness and higher purpose. Architectural grandeur may help, as can the sublime aspects of nature. You probably shouldn't select a holiday destination, which can suggest leisure, fun and a carefree state of mind. These are lovely, of course, but deeply at odds with what you are doing at a wedding: preparing to stick with someone through immense hardships.

What is vital is that the setting speaks of eternity, that it implies the smallness of our momentary concerns and encourages the mind to rise to the long term.

Lighting might usefully be subdued, suggesting how little we know ourselves or what we're getting into. It should highlight the couple, leaving them dramatically conspicuous in front of the audience. During the ceremony, the couple should be on a raised platform, together with the marriage director. They should be deeply conscious of being seen: this is not a private moment.

Clothes

Your clothes must be very formal, so as to stress the distance between this occasion and the ordinary habits of daily life. This is not the moment to express your individuality – crucially, marriage requires the repression of certain aspects of your singularity for the sake of harmony. In the ceremony, you are announcing your willingness to compromise, to adapt, to subordinate an intimate preference for the sake of what will work for your partner. A slightly anonymous suit or dress – such as might be worn by many others on their wedding day – indicates that you are ready to rein in your own desires. You might put on a cravat even if you feel it is a touch ridiculous, or a long gown, even though it's 'not you'. In much harder ways, you are going to have to repeat such acts of accommodation in the marriage as a whole.

At what time of day should the ceremony take place?

The rationale for the time of day is not the expression of your nature. It should be a time that is convenient for other people, irrespective of whether or not it is convenient for you. If you feel that it is boring and conventional to get married at 3 p.m. on a Saturday, that's probably a very good time to select. If you usually laze about on the weekend, 11 a.m. on a Sunday could be the perfect choice.

The guests

The guests are the public witnesses of your vows. Ideally, you'd feel deeply embarrassed to break your commitment to each other after so many people have seen and heard you making it. You don't just need your close friends, because they will usually be indulgent to your failings. You need a relatively intimidating audience: people who have travelled a long way; people you are slightly in awe of; people whose good opinion is important to you; people who are a bit sceptical of you. You might ask along some senior people from work (especially if you are not personal friends with them), a teacher from your school days that you admired and for whom you wanted to do your best, a crotchety aunt or a forbiddingly impressive friend of your parents. The point is that you should feel uncomfortable at the prospect of quitting the relationship after having said, in front of them, that you never would.

There is a growing trend, often driven by financial concerns, towards slightly smaller weddings, but a big crowd is, in fact, supremely important (even if the budget only stretches to a sandwich for them later). One needs a maximum number of people so as to cause the greatest possible embarrassment in years to come at the idea of having to call them all up and announce news of divorce. The larger the crowd, the slower one will be to pick up the phone. This gives due recognition to an important fact about marriage: it is a social institution, in which we often stay for reasons that go far beyond our own emotional desires. It involves us, but it's not just about us. It is about the dog, the children, the grandparents, the friends who got married in imitation of us and whose own relationships would suffer if we split. This sense that the marriage isn't just about us should come as a huge source of relief: there is nothing harder than being required to be happy in and for ourselves. There is a huge benefit in knowing that we will, with time, be living for others and that our own frame of mind won't always be the point.

The marriage director

The marriage director is the person who conducts the ceremony. Their role is to be an ambassador for noumenal time, for the idea that on this day you are publicly making commitments and assertions that aim to speak for the whole of your life. What you say at the ceremony will be relevant in ten or twenty years. Should you have children, your words will matter across the span of their lives too.

In their comments and conversation, the director shouldn't make reference to current events; they shouldn't make topical jokes; they shouldn't try to lighten the mood. They shouldn't be jolly or especially cheerful. Ideally, they will have a careful, sober and calm demeanour: they know that what you are doing is difficult and will at times seem too difficult. They know there will be rages and sulks; there will be bitter rows late at night, tears, accusations, cold looks, snide comments, intransigence, maddening disappointments and long-festering hurts on both sides. They are not cynical or weary: they believe deeply in the value of marriage, not because it is lovely (they know it isn't) but because its sorrows and pains are connected to a magnificent attempt to love another person and to become a properly mature version of oneself. When they ask you if you are willing to marry this person, they know full well what they are asking for – and they want to be sure you know it too. They will have something of the gravity and kindness of a radiologist who thinks you can be cured, but knows you face a lengthy and grim sequence of treatments. They are filled with pity and tenderness. They are not pretending it's going to be nice, but they are sure you should go ahead.

A central task of the marriage director is to get the audience to feel the gravity of the moment. Many present will be married or have been married or will get married one day. They will all know (in their own way) what marriage is really like, and the director has to summon the truth to the front of their minds – just as at a funeral, the covert central fact is that everyone has death to deal with, not simply the person laid out in the coffin.

The director's appearance should signal their attitude: they should wear elegant but serious black clothes and formal, highly polished and solemn shoes.

Music

Music plays an important role across the ceremony. It is the most effective mechanism for creating a mood, for getting us into a state in which certain kinds of thoughts and feelings more easily enter our minds. What matters isn't so much the exact pieces that are chosen as the outlook they support and encourage. We here define the mood the music should create rather than seeking to name specific songs or pieces.

ii. The Musical Prelude

As the guests enter the ceremonial space, solemn, ethereal music is played. It should be loud enough to encourage meditative silence in the audience. It is threshold music: we are leaving the familiar world of day-to-day concerns; there can be no more gossiping or cheery chat about parking. The mood is grave and solemn: something very sombre and serious is about to unfold.

After a few minutes, as the music comes to an end, the director enters and walks slowly to the platform and sits facing the audience. On a small table close to the director's chair are two small books, two photographs and two rings; these will play important roles in the ceremony.

The two people who are going to be married are, at this point, seated well away from the platform and as far from each other as possible.

iii. The Vows

What follows are the full ceremonial vows with instructions (indicated in italics) and suggested readings.

The vows are structured in three parts: Humility, Charity and Re-enchantment.

The Introduction

The music ceases. The director stands up and says:

Director

A wedding marks the attempt to unite two lives.

Experience makes it clear that a married couple face many problems; people who love and care for one another will fall into conflict over issues large and small; they will struggle to understand one another and they will be irked and dismayed by multiple features of each other's character.

Over the course of this marriage (as over the course of all marriages), there will be resentments, rows, secrets, sorrows, times of boredom and vales of anxiety.

A good marriage is not one from which troubles are magically absent; it is one in which troubles are faced with insight and generosity.

Love is not simply a feeling. It is a set of skills, including the skill of keeping in mind that our partner's most upsetting characteristics are rooted in their past sufferings and that they are expressions of hurt rather than indifference or viciousness. Love is the skill to forgive the wrongs done to us and the refusal to hoard them up as debts for eventual repayment. Love is the skill of seeing clearly our own flaws and failings – and hence of recognising, with gratitude, the generosity our partner displays daily in remaining beside us. It is the skill of understanding that everyone is deeply imperfect and of recognising, therefore, that we are meeting in our partner the faults of human nature, rather than the exceptional failings of one person.

This wedding ceremony marks a moment of public commitment. We, the congregation, are of supreme importance. We are being asked to hear what ... and ... say to one another today and to hold them to what they have openly asserted before us. There will be troubled times ahead when their own wisdom will fall prey to passion and to error. Our presence is designed to give them the love and the courage required for them to live up to their highest selves.

The couple are invited onto the stage.

They come from different directions, as separate people who are approaching one another. They stand either side of the director, facing the assembled guests.

The Ritual of Humility

Director

Humility is perhaps the most important emotion for the success of a relationship. Humility starts with an ample, accurate and sorrowful recognition of all one's failings. It is filled with apology and modesty. It doesn't pretend that flaws are charming quirks or excusable oddities. It contains an open admission that we wish we were different – and better.

Humility carries a shamed apology: I am genuinely and truly sorry for what and who I can sometimes be.

Humility carries an implication of gratitude: I'm profoundly grateful that – given what I am at points – you are willing to share a life with me.

Humility is not one-sided. Each person is damaged and difficult in different ways. The fate of the marriage hangs upon the willingness of each party to admit with grace, on repeated occasions, their own deep and serious inadequacies.

The director turns to one member of the

couple, partner 1, and asks:

Do you admit that you are a failed, broken human being – not in every way, but in some ways so serious that you will at points be a grave burden to …?

Partner 1   Yes, I admit this. I am failed and broken.

Director   Do you admit that you can be an extraordinary challenge, that you can be deeply difficult?

Partner 1   I admit this.

Director   Before coming here today – freely and openly and after careful reflection – you have listed your failings as you recognise them. You have listed them in this book – your own Book of Imperfections. Would you now, before me, your partner and your guests, read some of what you have stated in your own words?

The director points to two volumes on a small table. They are Books of Imperfection, elegantly bound volumes, clearly designed to be kept for a lifetime. Inside, each partner has written up a detailed list of their own failings, infelicities, quirks, shortfalls of maturity and ugly habits.

Partner 1 picks up their volume and reads a short extract.

(For example: I acknowledge that I can be rigid and cold; I goad and needle. Sometimes I'd rather make you unhappy than let you see and understand my own sorrow. When I get upset I become harsh and cutting.)

The director thanks the first partner, then turns to the second.

Director	Do you admit that you are a failed, broken human being – not in every way, but in some ways so serious that you will at points be a grave burden to …?
Partner 2	Yes, I admit this. I am failed and broken.
Director	Do you admit that you can be an extraordinary challenge, that you can be deeply difficult?
Partner 2	Yes, I admit this.

Director	Before coming here today – freely and openly and after careful reflection – you have listed your failings as you recognise them. You have listed them in this book – your own Book of Imperfections. Would you now, before me, your partner and your guests, read some of what you have stated in your own words?

Partner 2 reads a short extract from their book.

The director thanks the second partner.

The director asks the couple to exchange books.

The director addresses the audience:

There is nothing odd about this couple beyond the ordinary oddness that is everyone's lot. They have merely put into words the errors and failings of which we are all continuously guilty.

The Audience	We are all broken. We have all been idiots and will be idiots again.

We are all difficult to live with: we sulk and get angry, blame others for things that are our own responsibility, have strange obsessions and fail to compromise.

We are here to try to make you less lonely with your failings. We will mostly never know the details. But we understand.

We understand.

There now follows the first reading, which expands on the idea of humility and its constructive role in marriage.

Suggested First Reading

The failings of our partners can be deeply galling. We look upon their faults and wonder why they are the way they are.

At moments of particularly acute agitation, we need to rehearse an idea called the Weakness of Strength. This dictates that we should always strive to see our partner's weaknesses as the inevitable downside of certain merits that drew us to them, and from which we will benefit at other points – even if none of these benefits are apparent at present. What we are seeing are not their faults, pure and simple, but rather the shadow side of things that are genuinely good about them. We're picking up on weaknesses that derive from strengths.

In the 1870s, when he was living in Paris, the American novelist Henry James became a good friend of the celebrated Russian novelist Ivan Turgenev, who was also living in the city at that time. Henry James was particularly taken by the unhurried, tranquil style of the Russian writer's storytelling. He obviously took a long time over every sentence, weighing different options, changing, polishing, until – at last – everything was perfect. It was an ambitious, inspiring approach to writing.

But in personal and social life, these same virtues could make Turgenev a maddening companion. He'd accept an invitation to lunch; then – the day before – send a note explaining that he would not be able to attend; then another saying how much he looked forward to the occasion. Then he would turn up – two hours late. Making arrangements with him was a nightmare. Yet his social waywardness was really just the same thing that made him so attractive as a writer. It was the same unwillingness to hurry, the same desire to keep the options open until the last moment. This produced marvellous books – and dinner party chaos. In reflecting on Turgenev's character, Henry James noted that his Russian friend was exhibiting the 'weakness of his strength'.

Every strength that an individual possesses brings with it a weakness of which it is an inherent part. It is impossible to have strengths without weaknesses. Every virtue has an associated weakness. Not all the virtues can belong together in a single person.

This should subtly alter the way we see the defects and weakness of our partners. Our minds tend to hive off the strengths and see these as essential, while deeming the weaknesses freakish superfluities; in truth, the weaknesses are part and parcel of the strengths.

We must overcome the unhelpful idea that – if only we looked a little harder – we would find an unbroken soul. If strengths are invariably connected to failings, there won't be anyone who is remotely flawless. We may find people with different strengths, but they will also have a new litany of weaknesses. Human beings are not made for, and therefore should never aspire to, perfection.

To close the ritual, a short piece of music can be played, which condenses the themes of humility. The mood should be openly sorrowful and plaintive.

The Ritual of Charity

Director

In your life together, both of you will inevitably do many things that will upset and distress the other. It will be normal to be angry, to sulk, to be tempted to have an affair. You will condemn, you might gossip about the faults of the other; you will blame them for your sorrows; you will accuse them rather than take responsibility for yourself. When they act badly (as they will), you will often interpret them harshly; you will impute the worst motives to them.

The director invites the partners to repeat the following statements:

The couple

I will try not to malign you.

I will try not to have an affair.

I will try to understand what you attempt to communicate to me and not always merely pick up on the words you use, which may be meaner or more brusque than you intend.

I will try to explain my worries calmly

and without accusations.

When I fail, I will try to admit my errors without turning on you.

Director

Charity is at the heart of love. Charity means finding the least alarming, least panicked view of why the other is acting as they are. It sees the fear behind the aggression; it sees the loneliness at the root of a sulk; it recognises how shame can make a person defiant and how a hidden worry can unleash excessive harshness.

To both partners:

Will you now exchange the ritual gifts of charity?

Each partner gives the other a framed photograph of themselves as a child. The photographs are beautifully framed; they are important gifts.

The director explains what is going on:

The couple are exchanging photographs of themselves from childhood. We naturally act towards a child with a spirit of love that we often find it hard to adopt towards adults. This exchange of childhood images symbolises a commitment to treat one another with the kindness we wouldn't hesitate to show a child but so often refuse grown-ups.

The couple I will place this child version of you at the centre of my love. I will try to see your faults as a consequence of troubles in your past. I will look after the broken child within you.

The audience When with a child, we feel charity.

We don't rush to blame.

We look for attenuating circumstances.

We're slow to anger.

We're quick to forgive.

Your partner was a child – and they are still somewhere the same person they once were.

When you shout, you are shouting at this child.

When you betray, you are betraying this child.

When you blame, you are blaming this child.

The photo urges patience, tolerance and warmth.

Director	We will now hear the second reading.

Suggested Second Reading

At its most basic, charity means giving someone something they need but can't get for themselves. Normally this is understood to mean something material. We overwhelmingly associate charity with giving money. But, at its core, charity goes far beyond finance. It is about the interpretation of motives. It involves seeing that another person's bad behaviour is not a sign of wickedness or sin, but is a result of suffering. The psychologically charitable feel inwardly 'fortunate' enough to be able to come forward with explanations of others' misdeeds – their impatience or over-ambition, rashness or rage – that take attenuating circumstances into account. They generate a picture of who another person might be that can make them seem more than simply mean or mad. In financial matters, charity tends always to flow in one direction. The philanthropist may be very generous, but they normally stay rich; they are habitually the giver rather than the recipient. But in our relationships with others more broadly, the need for charity is unlikely ever to end up being one-sided, for we all stand in need of constant and shifting generosity of interpretation.

We are never far from requiring help in explaining to the world why we are not quite as awful as we seem.

Small children sometimes behave in stunningly unfair and shocking ways: they scream at the person who is looking after them, angrily push away a bowl of animal pasta, throw away something you have just fetched for them. But we rarely feel personally agitated or wounded by their behaviour. And the reason is that we don't assign a negative motive or mean intention to a small person. We reach around for the most benevolent interpretations. We don't think they are doing it in order to upset us. We probably think that they are a bit tired, or their gums are sore, or they are upset by the arrival of a younger sibling. We have a large repertoire of alternative explanations ready in our heads – and none of these lead us to panic or get terribly agitated.

This is the reverse of what tends to happen around adults in general, and our lovers in particular. Here we imagine that others deliberately have us in their sights. They probably relish the thought of causing us distress. But if we employed the infant model of interpretation, our first assumption would be quite different: maybe they didn't sleep well last night and are too exhausted to think straight; maybe they have a sore knee; maybe they are doing the equivalent of testing the boundaries of parental tolerance.

It's very touching that we live in a world where we have learnt to be so kind to children: now we must learn to be a little more charitable towards the childlike parts of one another.

The ritual of charity closes with a short piece of music: the mood should be oceanic, gentle, tender. It might have qualities in common with a lullaby.

The Ritual of Re-enchantment

The director introduces the third and final ritual:

Director

This couple has been drawn together because of what they admire and appreciate in one another. But it is normal that over time, under the pressure of daily life, their attractive and endearing qualities will grow obscure. They will forget the privilege of having been let into one another's lives. We acknowledge the risk head on, and attempt to avert it.

The couple

The good things about you will fade from my mind.

I will forget, under the pressure of our crowded calendars, the wondrousness of you.

We will be buried under administration, we will be preoccupied by points of disagreement.

At times, we'll see only what is wrong with someone we once cherished.

Director	The lovely, fascinating, sweet and impressive qualities that you have seen in one another will always continue to exist – even when they are lost from sight in times of stress, lassitude and rage.
	I want to direct your attention to a part of you that it was once particularly tender to have the right to touch. Please take hold of one another's right hands.
	The partners hold each other's right hands.
Director	This was the hand that, when you were initially granted permission to touch it, left you filled with excitement and wonder.
	It is the same hand. Its unique arrangement of lines and creases remains the same. The gaps between the fingers, the quirks of the veins and nails – these are places where an especially private kind of autobiography is inscribed.
	Look into each other's eyes. Vow to stay loyal to what a held hand symbolises: tenderness, mutual respect, appreciation.

Repeat after me: I will vow to keep looking at this person with all the wonder they deserve.

The couple I will vow to keep looking at this person with all the wonder they deserve.

Director I will try to see what I could see at the beginning.

The couple I will try to see what I could see at the beginning.

Director It was an unprecedented gift when they first let me hold this hand; it remains the same privilege today.

The couple It was an unprecedented gift when they first let me hold this hand; it remains the same privilege today.

There is silence for a few moments.

Director It is time for a third and final reading.

Suggested Third Reading

After being together with someone for a few years, their attractions stand to become grievously familiar. We will ignore them and become experts on their most trying dimensions. But we are never without a chance to reverse the process. It might be that we watch them when they are with friends. We pick up again on their shy smile, their sympathetic look, or the purposeful way they push back the sleeves of their pullover. Or perhaps we hear that a casual acquaintance thinks that they are fascinating and elegant and – mixed in with a dose of jealous irritation – via this potential rival's eye, we see again all that we could conceivably lose.

We are adaptable creatures. Disenchantment is not a one-way street. We are capable of a second, more accurate look. We can turn to art for hints on how to perform the manoeuvre of re-enchantment. Many works of art look with particular focus at what has been ignored and taken for granted. In the 18th century, the French painter Chardin didn't paint the grand things that other painters of the period went in for: heroic battles, majestic landscapes or dramatic scenes from history. Instead he looked around him and portrayed the quiet, ordinary objects of everyday life: kitchen utensils, a basket of fruit, a teacup. He brought to these objects a deeply loving regard. Normally you might not have given them a moment's thought. But, encouraged by Chardin, we start to see their allure. He's not pretending; he's showing us their real but easily missed virtues.

He isolates them, he concentrates attention, he carefully notes what is worthy of respect. He re-enchants our perception.

In the 19th century, the English painter John Constable did something similar for clouds. Nothing, perhaps, sounds duller. Maybe as children we liked to watch the grey banks of cloud drift and scud across the arc of the sky. We had favourites among them; we saw how they merged and separated; how they were layered; how a blue patch could be revealed and then swiftly covered. Clouds are lovely things, we once knew. Then we forgot. Constable's many cloud paintings remind us of the ethereal poetry unfolding above our heads at all moments, ready to delight us when we have the imagination to look up.

Imagine meeting your partner through the lens of art. You would find again the allure of things about them that – through familiarity and haste – had been neglected. We could study once more the magic of a palm that we once longed to caress; we could attend again to a way of tilting the head that once seemed so suggestive. In the early days, we knew how to see. Now as artists of our lives – in our own fashion – we can rediscover, we can select, refocus, appreciate. We can become the explorers of lost continents filled with one another's overlooked qualities.

There now follows a short piece of music. The mood may be joyful surprise, perhaps starting in a more sombre way before the feeling lightens and clears.

The Exchange of Rings and the Spousal Vow

The director invites the audience to stand.

Director

Knowing all this, fearing all this, hoping all this, will you, in front of all of us, vow to wed each other? Will you agree to share your lives – with all the restraint and sorrow that will be involved, as well as the joy, the kindness and the friendship?

The director turns to the first partner and says:

At this moment, time is suspended; you are speaking now for all the times of your life. Are you willing to marry ...?

Partner 1

I am.

Director

The director turns to the second partner and says:

At this moment, time is suspended; you are speaking now for all the times of your life. Are you willing to marry ...?

Partner 2	I am.
Director	I invite … and … to exchange rings, symbols of mutual commitment, and proof of a willingness to limit their freedom for the greater freedom of love and of a vow to merge their joys and sorrows.
	An exchange of rings.
Director	I now declare you married.
	The couple kiss; it should be a solemn gesture.
	After a pause of a few moments, the director signals to the audience to say the following together:
The audience	We have heard your vows.
	We hope for you.
	We fear for you.
	We see in your hopes our own hopes.
	We see in your fears our own fears.

We won't be there in the darkness of night.

But think of us when it feels impossible.

We know.

We understand.

We have been in our own night.

You won't see us all here again.

But keep our spirit alive in your memories.

Our marriages were

Or are

Or will be

Very far from perfect.

But we can learn and recover and improve. May your wisdom increase.

May this marriage be enough.

With all our hearts we wish you the best.

The couple step down from the platform and walk out slowly, while a final piece of music is played. The closing music should be triumphant. The mood is one of confidence and joy. It speaks of obstacles overcome, pain transcended: spring after winter.

3

After

i. The Party

It is an option to throw a great party to say thank you to those who have come and witnessed the wedding. But it's not only a thank you – the point of the party is to help embed the principles of a good marriage, for yourselves, and for everyone who attends.

Conversation menu

When the guests are seated, they should be invited to have a special kind of conversation. Instead of simply chatting, they should discuss the nature and purpose of love. A conversation menu is provided alongside each plate. Every guest has to ask and answer the menu with at least one of their fellow guests.

Candid answers are almost certain to reveal how normal it is for good relationships to be difficult: this will help correct an overly rosy sense of what is usual and create a more reliable benchmark for our own experiences.

Conversation menu

What would you want to tell this couple (who just got married) about how to keep their love alive?

How have the relationships you witnessed as a child shaped your views of marriage?

What do you find attractive in the idea of marriage?

What do you fear about marriage (if you were to get married, or remarried)?

What's the trickiest relationship you've had?

In a spirit of mutual honesty, and under a vow of deep secrecy, what is difficult about your current (or most recent) relationship?

What would be lovely about being married to you?

What would be difficult about being married to you?

Advice on speeches

Speeches are an opportunity to understand marriage and the purpose of love.

From the parents on both sides

A parent has known this person from infancy. They knew them when they were gauche, vulnerable and entirely at the mercy of others. They understand who they were and in powerful ways still are. Parents are the agents of one particular kind of love. They loved this person when the love couldn't be equal. Here are some guidelines for such a speech:

Your child is an adult now. But for a long time they weren't. They're not simply the person they are today; they are still also the child they were. We need to know about the child.

In what ways were they endearing when they were little? Describe something you loved doing with them.

What difficult things did you have to do for them – things that were no fun at all but that you did out of love for them? You did so much (probably).

Perhaps a lot of the time, you did it with good will, but maybe not always. In what ways were you a bad parent? How did you fail them? What pressures in your life made you a problematic adult to be around? What might you do differently if there was another opportunity?

You are reminding everyone that love involves

sacrifice but also failure. We are imperfect beings, and cannot get by without ample forgiveness.

You don't have to be funny or very wise or give advice. Indeed, you should refrain from doing so. Jokes are especially problematic. You are here to provide information.

A speech about each partner by each partner
The aim is to explain some important things that you love and admire about your partner. You have decided to share a lifetime with them and this is an opportunity to tell them, others and most importantly yourself, as clearly as you can, what about them moves and impresses you.

Be honest rather than conventional. You might be attracted to things that aren't usually thought of as love-able. Focus on details. Maybe they sometimes have a slightly shy smile that speaks of an endearing aspect of their character usually hidden under a more competent and confident surface; perhaps they become almost comically serious in conversation about certain topics and all their earnestness, which you find thrilling, comes to the fore. Possibly they are careful about how they arrange their shoes and you see in this an expression of their desire to take good care of things – you included, maybe.

ii. Presents

The guests shouldn't just give a present; they should accompany it with an account of why their own marriage or relationships are difficult and why they are themselves awkward people to live with. The new couple will (at some point) be tormented by the idea that their relationship is especially difficult and strange. Nothing makes us happier than news of the troubles of others, as notes accompanying the presents should implicitly recognise.

At dark moments in the marriage, one can turn to these gifts and flip through descriptions of the marital troubles of friends and relatives – and come away feeling that one is cursed certainly, but – importantly – in no way alone.

If single guests are unable to produce such things, they should arrive with vouchers for couples' therapy, to contribute to the enormous sum that will have to be spent on therapy over the lifetime of any decent marriage.

iii. The Wedding Night

Unfortunately, tradition has encouraged the idea that the night of the wedding should be filled with heroic sex. This might happen, but there are plenty of reasons why it probably won't after the drama of the wedding and a long party and partly, as well, because stringent expectations are alien to sexual intensity.

But the idea that sex is crucial is obviously not wrong, and the basic motive is right: the first night should be devoted to helping the couple with their sex life.

The question is how to do this. The assumption has been that great sex is the goal. But realistically what the married couple is preparing for is a life together in which sex will often be less than great and in which – increasingly over the years – sex will fade from view almost entirely. Instead of being spontaneous, inventive, impassioned and constant, sex will almost inevitably end up being intermittent, guarded and fraught.

This isn't a lovely prospect; it's just what is very likely to happen. And the couple will have to cope with it, if their marriage is to be bearable. At this great symbolic moment – in the special night after the wedding – a couple should ideally make a series of vows around the attitudes they will try to adopt towards sex.

Wedding Night Vows

Vow one:
I understand that sometimes, perhaps tonight, sex will be disappointing; that there will be times when I am really longing for sex and you will be busy, probably with a book or a phone. I promise to try not to see this as your fault.

Vow two:
I admit that it is deeply unlikely that two people will be perfectly in harmony around what kind of sex they want. I promise to try not to see this as a special curse on us.

Vow three:
I admit that if there are children they will often claim our attention at the least convenient moments. Our love for them will quite possibly inhibit us sexually; we'll feel shy unleashing our stranger, more exciting desires, knowing how sweet and innocent they are. I promise to try to accept that if we have a child, it will change our sex life, probably for the worse, and I won't blame you.

Vow four:
I want you to know that I've been seriously turned on by you: I have found you profoundly exciting. Probably sex will eventually become rare; but I promise I'll try to remember how much lust there once was.

Vow five:
I understand that sex will often be only as good as it can be: it won't be everything I might fantasise it could be. I acknowledge that there will be areas of my sexuality that don't make sense to you; I promise I will try not to make you feel bad about this.

* * * *

The point of these mutual vows is not to diminish sexuality. By keeping the realistically bad prospects in view and anticipating them, they give a couple a better chance to find the best sex they can together. The danger isn't that there will be challenges: that is inevitable. It is that the challenges will be seen as unfair and unreasonable and that resentment will build up to disastrous levels. The wedding night and its vows are aimed at reducing rancour.

iv. The Wedding Album

Wedding photographs are not simply a pleasing record of a special day: they have a bigger and deeper role. The aim of photos is to bottle the essence of what the wedding really signifies and make it available to us when we need it later. The task of the photographer is to create a series of works of art, made on many days, not all during the wedding itself, that can remind the couple of answers to some key questions:

Why did we get together?

We each have a long history. We may have to supply images of a gawky 15-year-old or a snapshot with a glamourous, disastrous ex. It might be useful to show images of our single lives: the messy kitchen sink or a picture of a lonely plate of beans, so as to remind ourselves that we weren't very happy living alone. We need these visual reminders because later we'll be internally harassed by the question: why did I marry you, why did we bind ourselves together, when there might have been so much easy fun elsewhere?

What virtues did we see in one another when we got married?

The images need to pick up on what charms us about each other. These might not be obvious things. The photographer needs to hear the themes of the wedding speeches from both partners and attempt to give these visual expression. There might be an image of one of you looking lost, or a close-up of an ankle, or of one of you wearing a large saggy jumper.

What impact does each person's family have on the relationship?

There should be special sections devoted to a visual analysis of each partner's broader family. It wouldn't seek to show them on the day, necessarily, but to reveal certain underlying characteristics: a charming but often overbearing mother; a sweet but not very confident father; a sister who was always that much more successful; a much loved brother who rebelled against the conventions of the world and paid a conspicuous price. These people have played major roles in forming our characters. We need to be constantly reminded of where we are each starting from.

How normal are marital problems in society at large?

In an utterly unconventional way, the wedding album should include images of other people – especially quite admirable-looking, interesting couples – in situations of despair and conflict. Their distress is not something to gloat about. It is a deeply necessary visual cue to bring us back to a realistic assessment of our own imperfect marriage. They are decent people and they are suffering.

This is what happens. Therefore, the tensions and frailties of our own union are represented (as they really are) as the normal tribulations that decent people experience when they share their life with another. The album becomes a resource against premature panic.

Looking back at one's 'wedding photos' in subsequent years would then take its place within the overall purpose of the wedding: it would help, in a small way, to persuade us to stay married.

v. Crises

There will be times when you will feel very bleak about your marriage. You will wonder why you ever got into the situation. You will feel you made a disastrous mistake in tying your life to this person. Those moments won't necessarily last long, but they are bound to arise – and we need to be prepared.

Here, therefore, is some consolation for the periods of agony.

Everyone, when known properly, is unbearable in some central ways

There is no one you could be married to that would not, at times, leave you feeling desperate. You too are tricky, you should remember.

Your sorrows are very normal

Many people are suffering in similar ways, and have done so in the past, and will do so again in the future. It's miserable, but you are participating in the common experience of humanity. Maybe they don't talk about it much, but millions would sympathise deeply with what you're going through. You feel completely alone, yet you are in a vast (shy) majority: a thoughtful, well-read surgeon screamed at his partner through the bathroom door late last night and woke the children. Right now, a level-headed, nicely dressed IT consultant lives in dread of her partner finding out she's been having an affair online.

Your worst thoughts are only thoughts

The feeling that you wouldn't mind if your partner were to die swiftly and painlessly, leaving you to start again, doesn't make you a monster: it's a very common thought that passes through the heads of obviously sane and reasonable people. It doesn't mean you wish your partner any harm. It will pass.

No one really understands anyone else

That your spouse doesn't grasp you in central ways is entirely unavoidable.

It's not strange if you would like to have an affair

It's reasonable and natural to want to. It would be wonderful to be wanted, to be held and loved and properly appreciated in bed. But an affair wouldn't solve the underlying issues, which have to do with frustration and a lack of connection.

Your heightened feeling of despair will probably pass quite quickly

Your anguish is very real at this moment. But later it

won't seem quite so bad. We get used to things. We cope better than we think. This too shall pass.

vi. Marriage Therapy

At present, marriage therapy is widely seen as a thing you do because you have a bad marriage: it is an admission of guilt or an announcement of hopelessness. It should rather be understood as a proper and reasonable support for a good marriage. It is the single greatest tool we can make use of to prevent a marriage from falling into an endangered condition.

Marriage therapy works its magic because it is a safe forum in which to discuss issues that, when handled by the couple alone, can too easily spin into ill temper and recrimination. The feeling that we haven't been heard in too long is what prevents us from listening. But in a consulting room, a good therapist becomes the wise broker, allowing each person to have their say, sympathising with both parties, without taking either of their sides. Therapy becomes a safe diplomatic back channel, away from the conflictual atmosphere of domestic life. The therapist can help the couple to see that behind one person's rage is pain and a history of despair in childhood. Or they might make someone aware of what it feels like to be on the receiving end of hostile silence or controlling inquisitions. They can hold both parties back from one another's throats for just long enough that they may start to understand what their previously caricatured opponent is going through.

One of the key tasks of the therapist is to expose us often enough to a more sane, respectful, reasonable and realistic outlook than our own. The therapist's kindly, wise voice should become our own. We begin to intuit what they would have said in a given situation and, when they are no longer there, can learn to say some of the important, calming and kind things to ourselves at moments of crisis and loneliness.

Far from a self-indulgence, undergoing therapy is one of the most generous things we could ever do for all those who have to live around us. Those who have spent time in therapy are ever so slightly less dangerous to be around, a little better able to warn those who depend on them of how frustrating and peculiar they might sometimes be. We owe it to ourselves, and just as importantly, those who love us, to take our courage in our hands – and to 'see someone' throughout our marriage.

Picture Credits

Cover   © Christopher Roberts

p. 20   Maison Carrée in Nîmes, France.
             tichr / Shutterstock

p. 21   The High Altar of St Paul's Cathedral as
             viewed from the choir. Photo by: David
             Iliff / Wikimedia Commons. License:
             CC-BY-SA 3.0

Also available from The School of Life:

The Couple's Workbook

Homework to help love last

Therapeutic exercises to help couples nurture patience, forgiveness and humour.

Love is a skill, not just an emotion – and in order for us to get good at it, we have to practise, as we would in any other area we want to shine in.

Here is a workbook containing the very best exercises that any couple can undertake to help their relationship function optimally – exercises to foster understanding, patience, forgiveness, humour and resilience in the face of the many hurdles that invariably arise in a relationship.

The goal is always to unblock channels of feeling and improve communication. Not least, doing exercises together is – at points – simply a lot of fun. No one can be intuitively good at relationships. We all need to do some homework to become the best partners we can be.

ISBN: 978-1-912891-26-9

£18 | $24.99

The Good Enough Parent

How to raise contented, interesting and resilient children

A parenting guide providing compassionate instruction and insight into raising a resilient well-balanced child.

Bringing up a child to be an authentic and mentally robust adult is one of life's great challenges. It is also, fortunately, not a matter of luck.

The Good Enough Parent is a compendium of life lessons, including how to say 'no' to a child you adore, how to look beneath the surface of 'bad' behaviour to work out what might really be going on, how to encourage a child to be genuinely kind, and how to handle the moods and gloom of adolescence.

Most importantly, this is a book that knows that perfection is not required – and could indeed be dangerous, because a key job of any parent is to induct a child gently into the imperfect nature of everything. Written in a tone that is encouraging, wry and soaked in years of experience, *The Good Enough Parent* is an intelligent guide to raising a child who will one day look back on their childhood with just the right mixture of gratitude, humour and love.

ISBN: 978-1-912891-54-2

£15 | $19.99

Also available from The School of Life:

How to Overcome Your Childhood

A guide to breaking free from the enduring, and sometimes damaging, behavioural patterns learnt in childhood.

To an extraordinary and humbling extent, who we are as adults is determined by events that happened to us before our fifteenth birthday. The way we express affection, the sort of people we find appealing, our understanding of success and our approach to work are all shaped by events in childhood.

We don't have to remain prisoners of the past, but in order to liberate ourselves from our histories, we must first become fully aware of them. This is a book about such a liberation.

We learn about how character is developed, the concept of 'emotional inheritance', the formation of our concepts of being 'good' or 'bad' and the impact of parental styles of love on the way we choose adult partners. We also learn about how we might evolve emotionally and how we may sometimes need to have a breakdown in order to have a breakthrough.

We are left with a powerful sense that building up an emotionally successful adult life is possible, so long as we reflect with sufficient imagination and compassion on what happened to us a long while back.

ISBN: 978-1-9999179-9-9
£12 | $16.99

The School of Life is a global organisation helping people lead more fulfilled lives. It is a resource for helping us understand ourselves, for improving our relationships, our careers and our social lives – as well as for helping us find calm and get more out of our leisure hours. We do this through films, workshops, books, apps, gifts and community. You can find us online, in stores and in welcoming spaces around the globe.

THESCHOOLOFLIFE.COM